INSTEAD of SCALES

SCALES

12 Cycles Of
Piano Warm-ups For
Smooth Running

by Robert Dumm

Dedicated To

*Kate Shanaphy, to give her
the "Piano Skates"
she wants and needs!*

JUST A WORD BEFORE YOU BEGIN—

"Instead of Scales" was written for a girl whose teacher gave her scales too soon! "Do your pieces and do your scales." After trying hard she felt confused and frustrated; she couldn't feel that scales were helping her to play. "What can I do *instead of scales?*" she wailed. To that girl, and to all others out there, big and little, who've cried out at the futility of a prescribed drill, here's our answer.

There's plenty to do *before* scales. Not that we disbelieve in the value of scales for piano playing. Scales in one form or another make up about half of all piano literature (the other half consists of chords and their derivatives). But we know that scales are often given to the new pianist before he or she has acquired the motor skills that smooth scales require. Once the pianist has taken some time to absorb those preparatory skills and has made them a part of his or her playing, smooth-running scales just seem to happen.

So here they are, the six prep skills you need, rotating in a dozen cycles: five-finger action, thumb-oil, hand relays and crossovers, five-finger rotations, hand-slides along the key surfaces and note-figures that, like Hanon's exercises, work through the tones of a full octave scale.

The exercises are carefully placed in the order of their difficulty, so all you need do is turn the pages, skipping nothing. They are made for fun in the doing, and for contrasts in musical mood and in the muscles you use. Work on two consecutive ones at a time. Work each one through several keys, and play them with both hands as soon as you know the pattern.

This is the symmetrical principle that quickly turns you into a two-handed pianist. Follow the fingerings, and above all, the dynamics and accents. For rhythm, the FEEL of muscular tension-release *in time* is the action that builds your skill.

Forget the words if you find them silly. But remember, the silliest words of all, nursery rhymes and TV commercials, are what dance and jingle into your head, never-to-be-forgotten! They give you a certain swing-along freedom that groups notes into phrases, and animates those phrases by spaced stresses.

So, off to your pianistic pushups. Make them a part of each and every day. By the time you've worked through the twelve cycles, you will find your hands running across the keyboard with the greatest of ease!

Cycle 1

BOOTS:

Follow the fingering to get the feel of a *step*, then a *skip* on the keys.

SNOWDROPS:

Let your hand dip and rise a little with each slur.

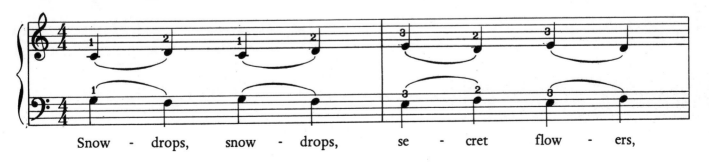

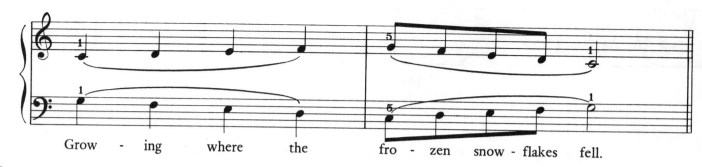

Grow - ing where the fro - zen snow - flakes fell.

3 THE SECRET DOOR:
Keep your 1,2,3,2,1 notes very steady from the beginning to prepare for a smooth five-finger run at the end of this workout.

Some - thing's hid - ing in the clos - et,

Take a peek and then you close it tight *shut!*

4 THE CRABWALK:
Let your finger tips be "in touch" as they smoothly cross each other.

5 MARCH WIND:
Cover and hold each five-finger pattern *before* you begin so that you will keep your place when the left hand crosses over the right.

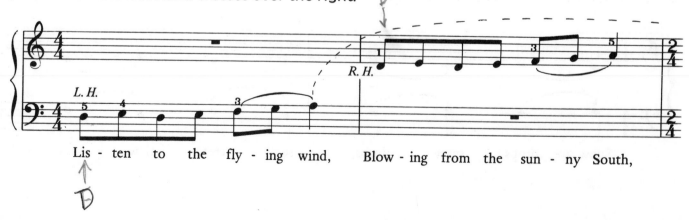

Lis - ten to the fly - ing wind, Blow - ing from the sun - ny South,

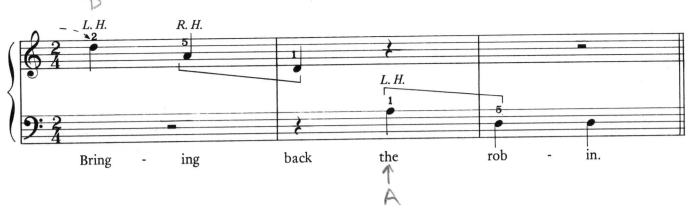

Bring - ing back the rob - in.

HIDE-AND-SEEK & PUSH-UPS:
Accent the first note of each slur to enliven the rotary action of your hand and forearm.

All - ee, all - eee, eve - ry - bod - y in - free;

All - ee, all - ee, Eve - ry - bod - y home.

Push - ups, push - ups, ear - ly in the morn - ing;

Push - ups, push - ups, Keep your tum - my flat!

7 **SOFT SQUASHES:**
After each "squash" (or cluster of notes), slide your thumb along the keys to reach the next hand position.

HALLOWEEN NIGHT:
The steady, moderate rhythm allows you to *press into* each key with equal force.

HALLOWEEN:
To develop better control of the outer, often weaker part of your right hand, stress the 5-3, 4-2 zigzag pattern.

(You may want to double this with *both* hands)

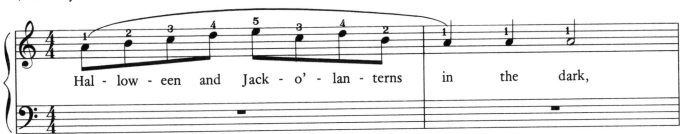

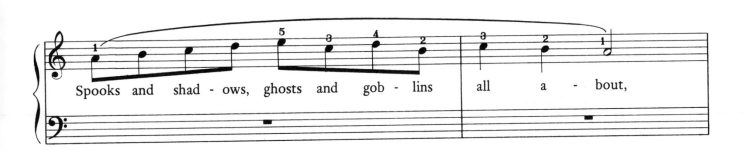

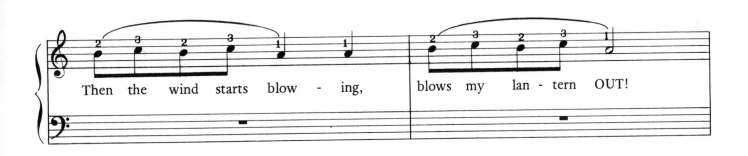

Can't you hear it howl - ing all a - round the park?

---

10 **CATERPILLAR:**

Emphasize each half note of the slower "snail" pattern to help coordinate your hands.

A slow "crawl"

"Snail"

---

11 **THE SIDE-STEP CRABWALK:**

Make your lazy thumb cooperate with the rest of your hand by letting it lightly touch the tip of the finger it is passing.

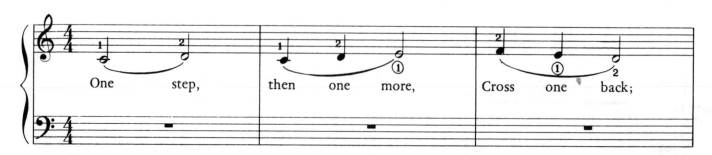

One step, then one more, Cross one back;

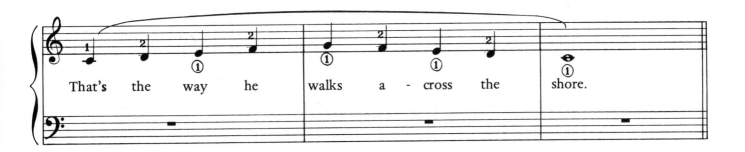

That's   the   way   he   walks   a - cross   the   shore.

2 **THE TWO OWLS:**
As the melody alternates between the right and left hand, keep the "listening" hand quietly in its place, so it is ready to "answer" back.

To - whit,   to - whoo!   To - whit,   to - whooo!   Who - o   are

you?   Who - o   are   you?   What   do   you   do?   Where   do   you

go?   What   do   you   do   in   my   dark   wood?   Where   do   you

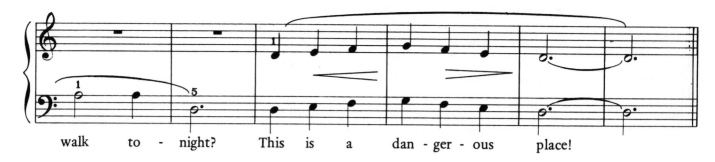

walk to - night? This is a dan - ger - ous place!

13 TOM, TOM THE PIPER:

"Plop" your hands together on the accented, staccato quarter note that starts each phrase. That will loosen your wrist for the smaller slurs that follow.

For Phrasing

Tom, Tom the Pip - er, He went out; up, up a big hill,

to the top. Up at the top he met a bear who did - n't like him

be - ing there! Run, run, run, run Fast - er, fast - er, till you're safe - ly home!

14 SILLY SONG:

Accent the *third* beat of each bar for a healthy rotary action of the hand. Play it briskly, not slowly.

Briskly

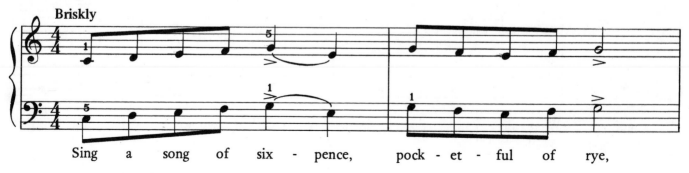

Sing a song of six - pence, pock - et - ful of rye,

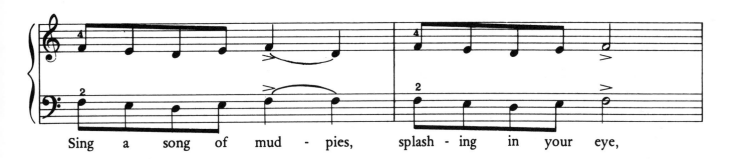

Sing a song of mud - pies, splash - ing in your eye,

Sing a song of pup - pies, roll - ing o - ver, up and o - ver, in a *heap!*

RUNNING THE COURSE:

Feel your hand bounce lightly as the thumb plays. This will "spring" your hand from position to position, which is necessary for playing scales smoothly later on.

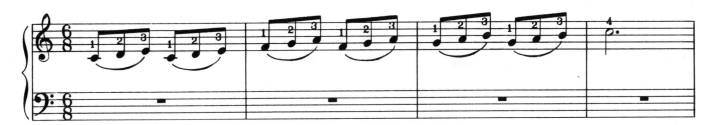

Cycle 3

16 **BEST FOOT FORWARD:**

Accent the skips of thirds in the second, fourth, and sixth bars, to articulate the different *feel* of *steps* versus *skips* on the keyboard.

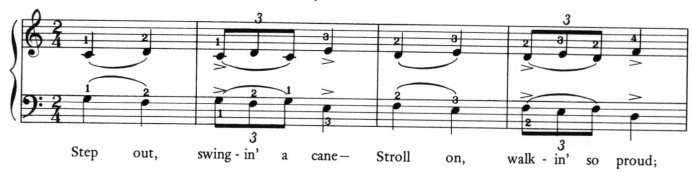

Step out, swing - in' a cane— Stroll on, walk - in' so proud;

Head high, sing - in' out loud— Put - tin' your best foot for - ward!

17 **DUCKS-IN-A-ROW:**

As the exercise progresses, drop your hands more freely on the thumbs that start each bar. This will loosen your thumb action and clarify your phrasing.

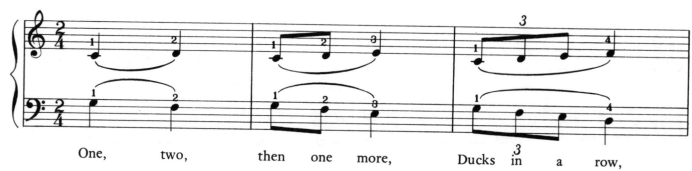

One, two, then one more, Ducks in a row,

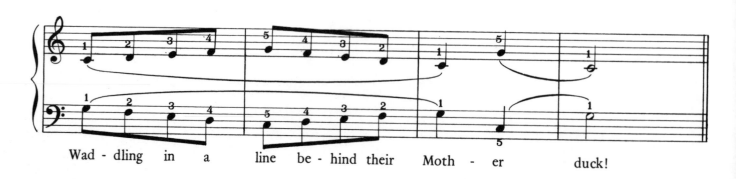

Wad - dling in a line be - hind their Moth - er duck!

8 **VALENTINE CANDY:**

For each phrase-group, let your hands drop smoothly at the beginning, then roll sideways for the following notes.

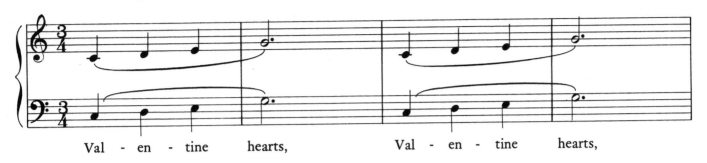

Val - en - tine   hearts,   Val - en - tine   hearts,

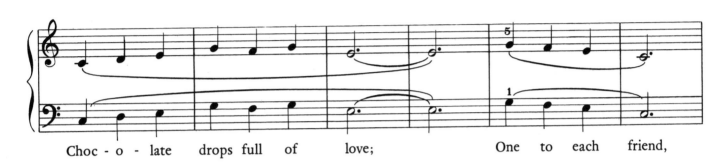

Choc - o - late   drops full   of   love;   One   to   each   friend,

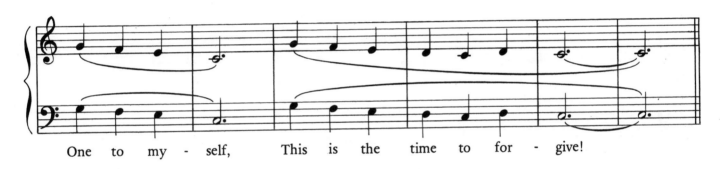

One   to   my - self,   This   is   the   time   to   for - give!

19 **LOBSTER WALK:**

Draw your hand smoothly and lightly over the keys as you "walk by threes." This is a valuable preparation for playing scales smoothly in the future.

20 **THE AUTUMN WIND:**
Keep your right hand in place throughout this workout. It will guide your left hand to a smooth crossing of three octaves.

(Whoo)_____ (Whoo)_____ It's on-ly wind in the

chim - ney; (Whoo)_____ (Whoo)_____ It sounds like hun-dreds of

voic - es cry - ing. It is the song of the wind.

21 **CHORD-BUILDERS:**
Equal stress on fingers *one* and *five* will make a clear "frame" for your chords.

DAISIES:

Always begin with the prep step: it helps your thumb guide your hand through the chord positions. When you play at two, center the weight of your hand over the single top tones of each chord, for swift side-shifting along the keys.

① Prep-set

The Bicycle Built For Two

② Front Seat:

"Dai - sy, Dai - sy, Give me your an - swer, Do!"

The Back Seat:

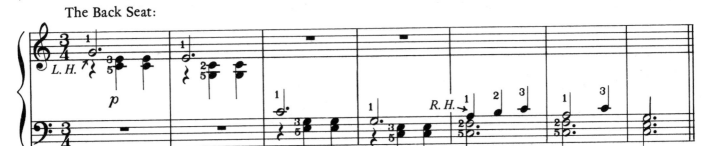

"Dai - sy, Dai - sy, Give me your an - swer, Do!"

BAY BRIDGES:

Play the pattern briskly and with a crescendo at each ending. Immediately move along to the next step of the scale. Keep *in your ear* the sound of your end-tone, one octave away from where you began. That is the musical "shore" you are reaching with your "bridge."

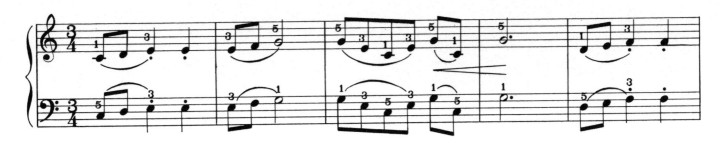

Play on each step

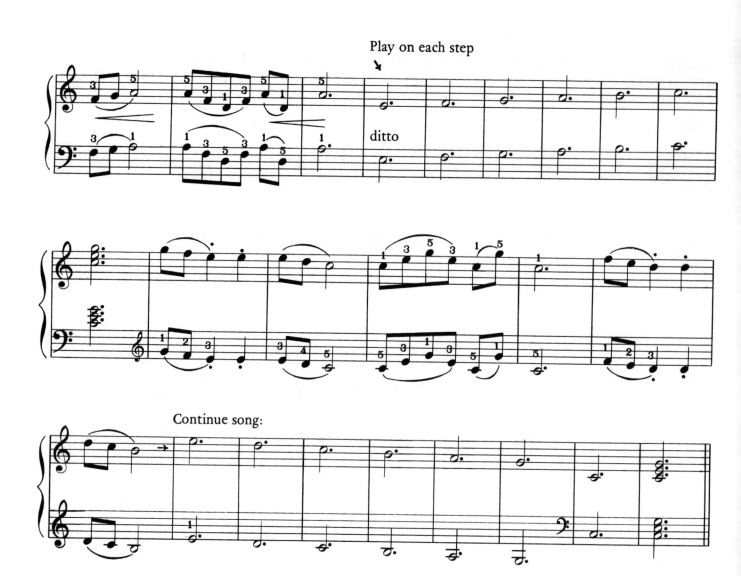

ditto

Continue song:

Cycle 4

SOUNDING THE (CHORD) COLORS
Play this work-out briskly to emphasize the changes in chord color. Drop both hands *into* the *first* notes of each bar, just as you lift the hand lightly for the last two beats.

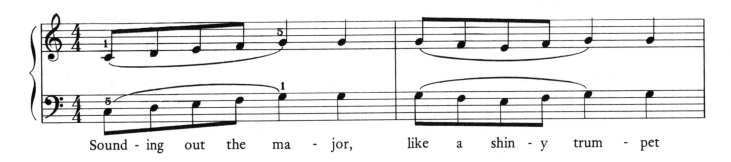

Sound - ing out the ma - jor, like a shin - y trum - pet

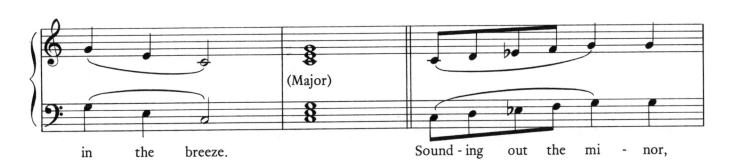

in the breeze. (Major) Sound - ing out the mi - nor,

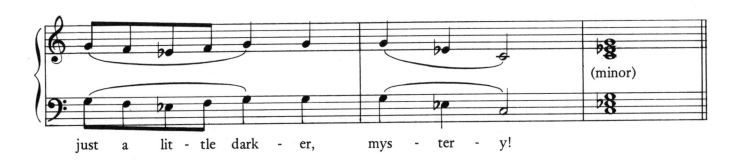

just a lit - tle dark - er, (minor) mys - ter - y!

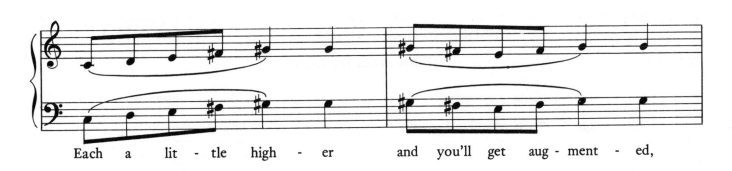

Each a lit - tle high - er and you'll get aug - ment - ed,

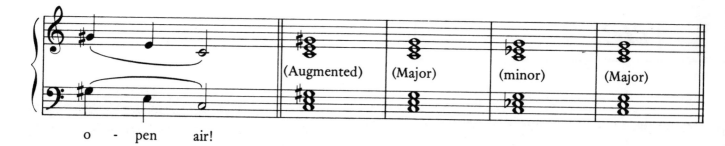

(Augmented)   (Major)   (minor)   (Major)

o - pen   air!

25 SLIDING ON THE ICE:

"Rap" the first notes of each bar with a sharp downward motion of both hands, so that their natural rebound will then lighten the notes that follow.

26 MAKING WAVES:

Drop freely into the *first* beat of each phrase, then let your hands rise to feel lighter as they run to the end of the phrase — as a splash in a still pond is followed by ripples.

(Ripplers and Breakers)

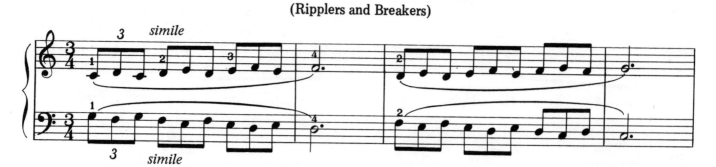

7 AT THE DOCTOR'S:

Drop the full weight of your hands onto your thumbs. This leaves your fingers free to "tap" with their weight alone.

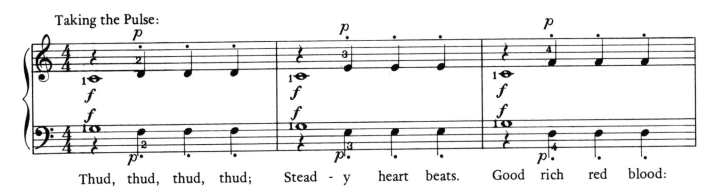

Thud, thud, thud, thud;   Stead - y   heart beats.   Good rich red blood:

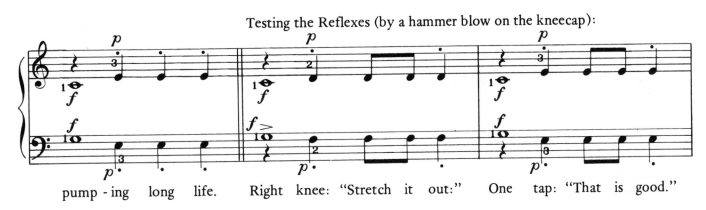

pump - ing long life.   Right knee: "Stretch it out:"   One tap: "That is good."

Left knee: "Give it here."   Two taps: "That's the stuff.   Keep   kick - ing."

28 **DIPPERS:**

Here, you must contrast a "big" dip of the wrist on beat one of each bar with a smaller, "little" dip on the second beat. This helps you bring out the natural stress of the 2/4 meter.

(Slurring as you go)

29 **FANFARE FOR THE COMMON CHORD:**

Play this one *Allegro,* accenting the start of each slur and the natural "liftoff" for each repeated note. This will both lighten and synchronize the action of your hands.

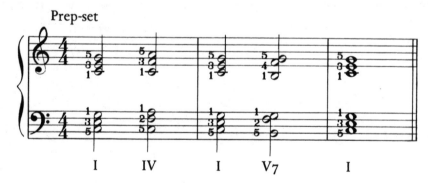

22

Fanfare ②

TETRACHORD SCALES:

First, place both hands over the keys they will play. As you hold the dotted half note, think ahead to what the other hand will play next. This workout shows you how to build scales before you actually begin to "practice" them.

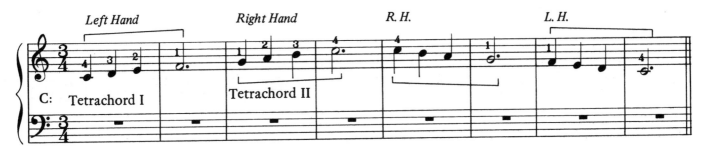

C: Tetrachord I   Tetrachord II

Now, L. H. plays what R. H. *just* played:

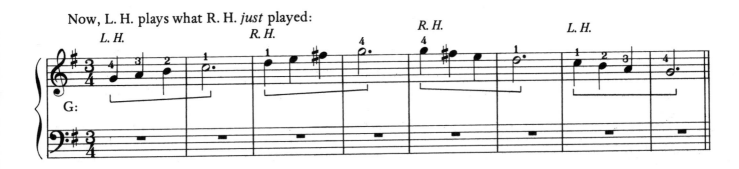

G:

Once again: L. H. begins where R. H. *just* played:

D:

Follow the same pattern for the following:

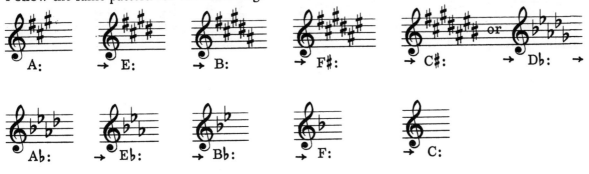

A: → E: → B: → F♯: → C♯: or Db: →

Ab: → Eb: → Bb: → F: → C:

FLIPPERS (RH & LH):

For this workout, edge sideways over the keys by groups of 3 and 4 notes, just as in scales.

(Right Hand)

(Left Hand)

Cycle 5

2

SAN FRANCISCO CABLECAR:

Carefully articulate the very *first* note of each slur. This exercise teaches you to make it clear, even when it occurs on the *weak* part of the beat.

For steps mixed with skips, all fingers.

Slow - ly up Nob. Hill it creeps, Pull - ing for - ward then fall back—

Start a - gain and say a prayer and Make it to the top, A - men, All right!

3

STEPS, SKIDS, AND SKIPS:

Here is valuable training in changing quickly from steps to skips. Try for special clarity in bars 6 and 8.

Two Steps, Then a slide, Down Two Skips. Two steps, then a slide,

skip and step. Slide back up; stand still, zig - zag down two keys.

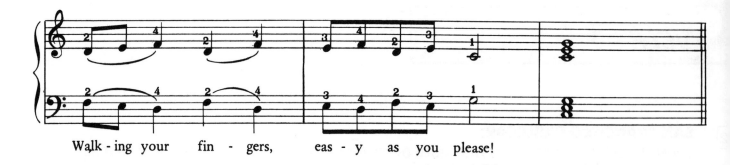

Walk - ing your fin - gers, eas - y as you please!

34 **AS THE WORM TURNS:**
Try here for a light and even finger action. Work this one carefully through all keys. It is the basic preparation for beautiful trills.

(Three Squirmers for Your Fingers)

① INCHWORM:

② EARTHWORM:

The worm turns. . .   *. . .and slithers forward. . .*

. . .and coils itself to sleep.

③ THOUSAND-LEGGER:

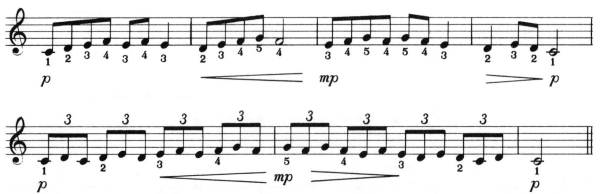

For the Left Hand, place your thumb on G and reverse each figure.

26

WALKING THE POODLE:

Lift both hands at the wrist to keep them light for the shifts of direction. Then, remember to keep the thumb lightly *in touch* with the back of the finger it is passing. After you practice with fingers 1 and 2, try 1 and 3, 1 and 4, and (on a good day) 1 and 5.

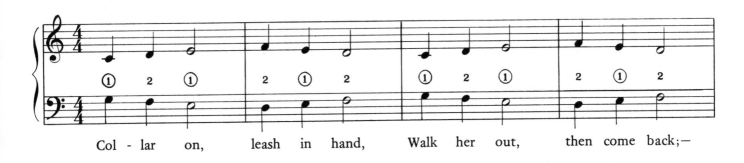

Col - lar   on,   leash   in   hand,   Walk   her   out,   then   come   back;—

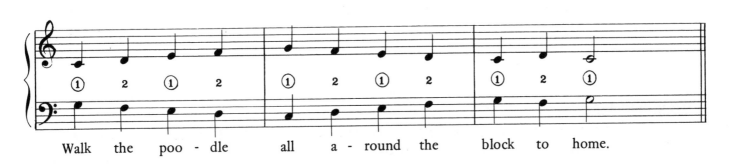

Walk   the   poo - dle   all   a - round   the   block   to   home.

BEAR TRACKS:

Always start with the chord sets so that your hands become familiar with the shapes of the chords. Then you are free to let your hands drop freely, like "paws" into the keys. Try for a big, full sound and stay in touch with the keys when your left hand crosses over.

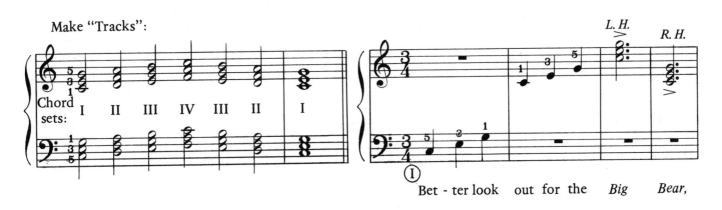

Chord sets: I   II   III   IV   III   II   I

Bet - ter look out for the *Big*   *Bear,*

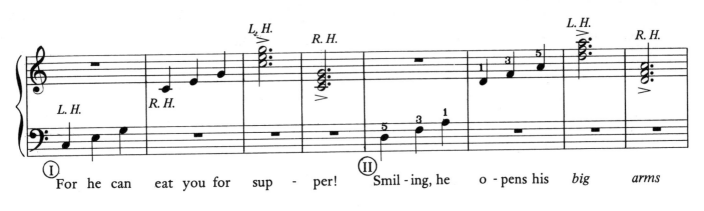

For he can   eat you for   sup - per!   Smil - ing, he   o - pens his   *big*   *arms*

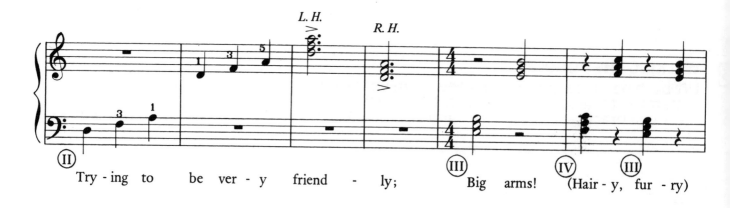

(II) Try - ing to be ver - y friend - ly; (III) Big arms! (IV) (Hair - y, fur - ry) (III)

(II) Big paws! (III) [War - y, war - y!] (II) He'll scoop you (I) up in a *big bear hug!*

37 **WASHING MACHINE:**

Play each downbeat with a strong accent to assure a free rotary back-forth roll of the hand. This will help shape the slurred groups.

Rub - a dub - dub, Rub - a dub - dub, Bub - bles of suds and soap,

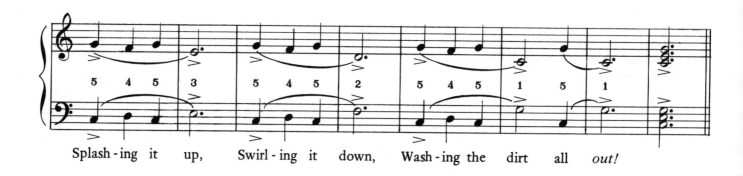

Splash - ing it up, Swirl - ing it down, Wash - ing the dirt all *out!*

28

ICE-SKATING:

Wherever you have a 5-1 or 1-5 connection, as between bars 1 and 2, link the two fingers carefully by touching at their tips. This *covers* the notes, and lets you become free to "glide over the keys with the greatest of ease."

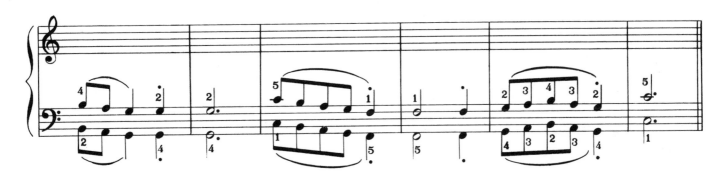

GAS-AND-BRAKES:

Be sure to move minimally in a straight line of the hand when you cross each bar to place the hand for the next bar. Observe, too, the small crescendo that ends each bar.

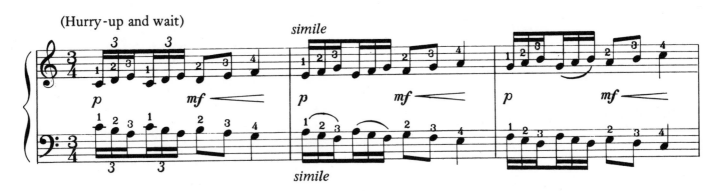

Cycle 6

RING-AROUND-THE-ROSEY:
Dotted notes often mean accents for the pianist. Play this exercise at a moderate tempo, so that you can accent each dotted note.

WARM-UP

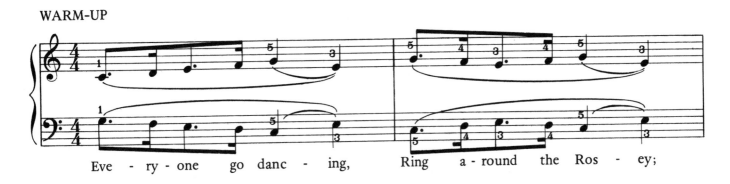

Eve - ry - one go danc - ing, Ring a - round the Ros - ey;

Pock - et - ful of pos - ies, we all fall down. (in a *heap!*)

THE ROYAL PAIR:
In bar 3 and similar places, lift your wrist and slightly detach the repeated notes, so that you can freely drop your hands onto the final half note chord. Try it in all keys.

Sound the gold-en trum-pet of the king chord: Sound the sil - ver trum-pet of the

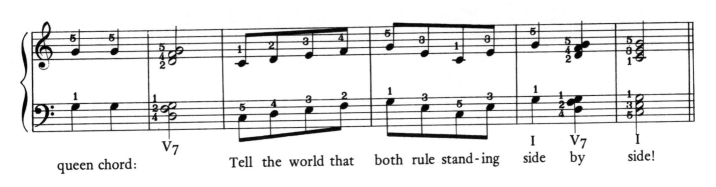

queen chord: Tell the world that both rule stand-ing side by side!

CHORD COLORS:

Accent the final notes of each phrase to bring out the color changes between major and minor. This exercise is as much ear training as it is finger training.

Major

Scale Steps: 1 ... 3 ... 5

Minor

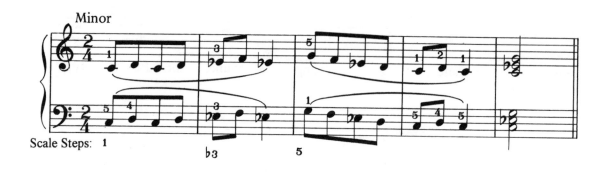

Scale Steps: 1 ... ♭3 ... 5

Diminished

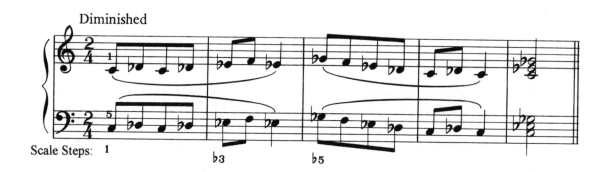

Scale Steps: 1 ... ♭3 ... ♭5

Augmented

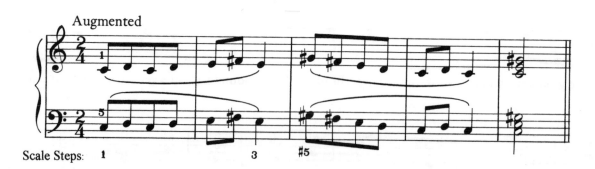

Scale Steps: 1 ... 3 ... ♯5

WAGTAILS:

In this exercise, the thumb is lured farther and farther underneath the hand. Keep it sliding along and *in touch with* the keys at all times.

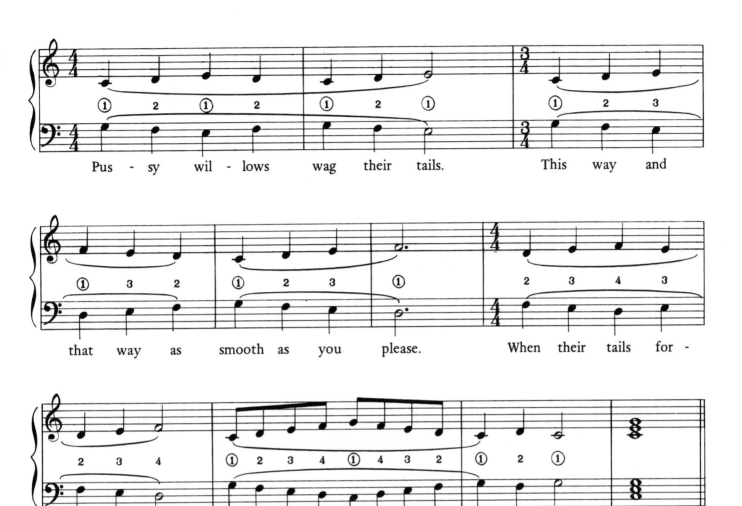

THE OLD BELL RINGER:

Once you've got both hands hanging in place, let them go loosely from the wrist for their back-and-forth relay action. The hand, not the fingers, produce the tone here.

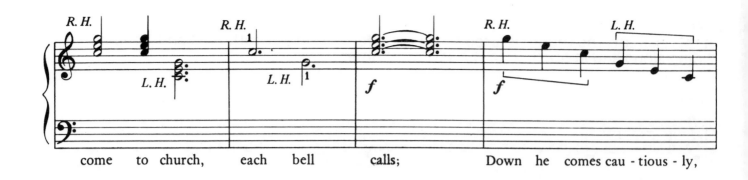

come to church, each bell calls; Down he comes cau - tious - ly,

(Organ and Choir)

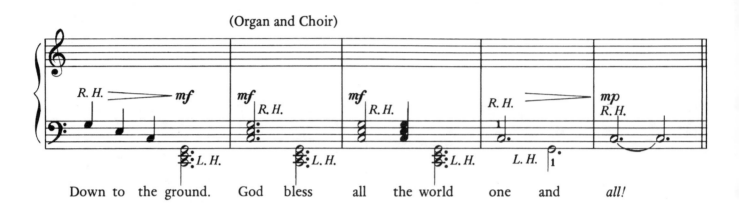

Down to the ground. God bless all the world one and *all!*

45 **THE LONE RANGER:**

Play most of this exercise *mp,* reserving full *forte* for its final chords. Play it fast, but with a clear accent to start each slur. That's what awakens the rotary action of the hand.

Here he comes rid - ing, beat - ing the bush - es, Hand-some and fear - less,

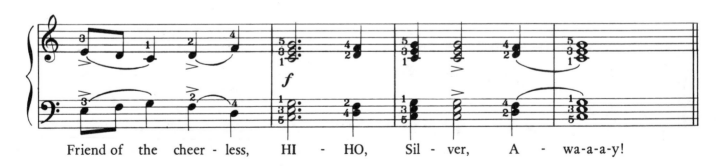

Friend of the cheer - less, HI - HO, Sil - ver, A - wa-a-a-y!

ROMP ON THE GRASS:

Do not play this exercise too quickly, and remember to drop onto the first note of each bar. It is this vigorous "springing" effect that loosens the hand and lets it change easily from a relatively closed to an open position.

Front - wards, back - wards, to and fro, Head - o - ver - heels,

Back - to - a - stoop, Till I roll o - ver in One Fell Swoop!

SCALE SLICES:

At the beginning of the exercise and before the repetition of the pattern, give a quick little rise of the wrist, like a conductor's upbeat. This instantly banishes muscular tension and gives you a fresh start. This wrist "upbeat" is as important to good piano playing as taking a breath is to a singer.

THE CREEPY-CRAWLIES:

Here is essential training in finger independence. As you use the weight of your hand to hold the long note, your other fingers are free to cross over in extreme legato.

Variation ① "Snail Stuck in Slime"

Left Hand:

Cycle 7

COZY SONG:

Since this exercise teaches you to "sing with your fingers," it is best to sing the melody either before or as you play. Try to increase the volume as the pitch rises, and decrease it as the pitch falls.

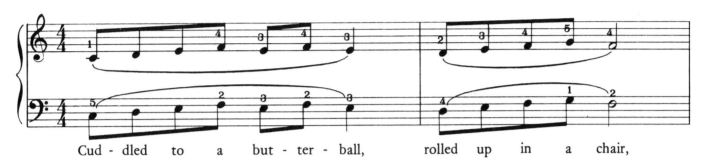

Cud - dled to a but - ter - ball, rolled up in a chair,

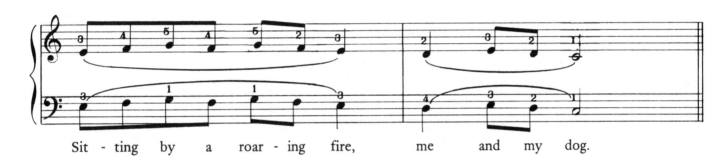

Sit - ting by a roar - ing fire, me and my dog.

APRIL SHOWERS:

By giving equal accents to the starting note of each slur, you will gain equal strength in the nail joint of each finger. But don't force that accent. Use what you know about rotary action to join the groups of slurred notes.

A - pril show - ers soak the ground so ten - der lit - tle flow - ers

Dot the mead - ows ev - 'ry - where, they make the spring-time smell so GOOD!

MAY FLOWERS:

Do not play this one fast. You need time to stress each beat a little and play down into the bed of the key action. This will synchronize the action of the hands and let you feel the beats still "bouncing" behind the faster eighth notes.

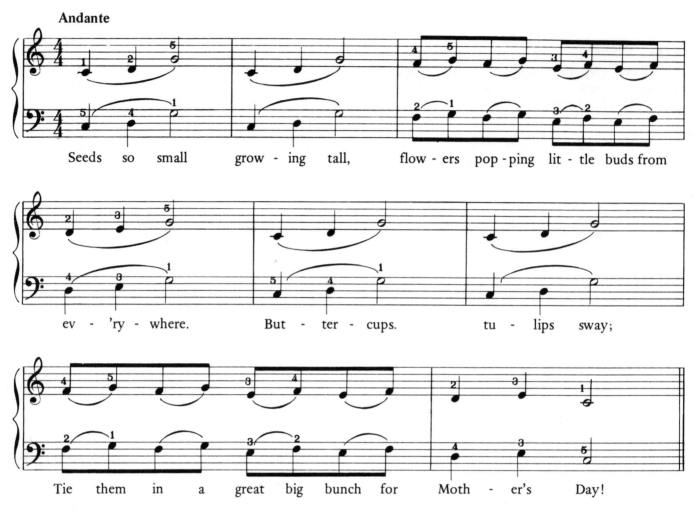

Seeds so small grow - ing tall, flow - ers pop - ping lit - tle buds from

ev - 'ry - where. But - ter - cups. tu - lips sway;

Tie them in a great big bunch for Moth - er's Day!

DOODLES:

By accenting the long notes of bar 2 and all similar places, you release the smaller "speed muscles" to work well for the groups of eighth notes. Keep them *p* (no more), but make the accented long notes *forte*.

(Watch Your Thumbs!)

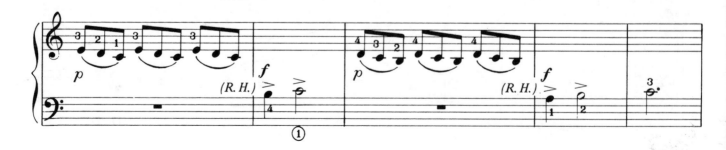

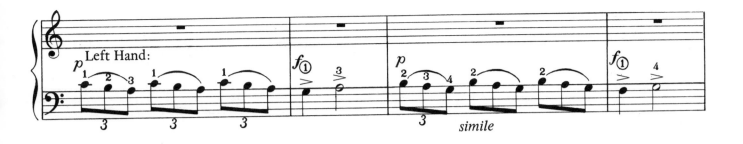

JACK FROST:

Keep the right hand *in place* after it has played. It serves as a marker, or reference point, for the traveling left hand. This is valuable experience in minimalizing motion.

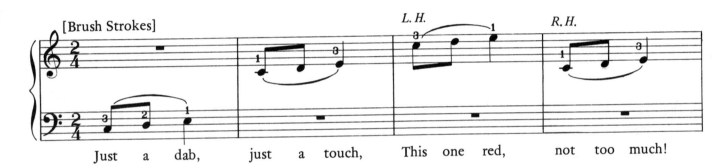

Just a dab, just a touch, This one red, not too much!

Col - or of gold. Up comes the au - tumn breeze, blow - ing so

cold! Down they come fall - ing all o - ver the town!

54 **GOLDEN TRUMPET:**

This exercise in refined rotation, if practiced very rhythmically, will teach your neighboring fingers the lightness they need for good trills.

Sound the horn, Blow it to the sky! Send its laugh-ing hap-pi-ness on

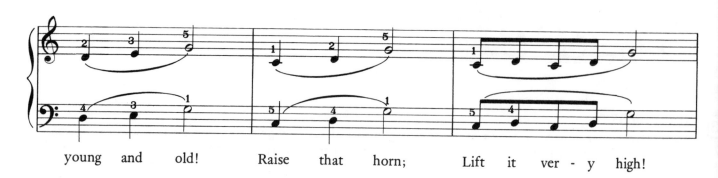

young and old! Raise that horn; Lift it ver-y high!

Let it spray its gold-en notes like lit-tle flakes of gold!

55 **ROCKERS:**

Accent every dotted quarter note with a bold sideways swing of your forearm. In this exercise, you proceed from hand-rotation to forearm rotation, another pianistic skill needed for rolled chords.

PINCERS:

Play the sixteenth notes softly, and the eighth notes with a marked accent. This will *swing* the hand past the link of 5 to 1 (or 1 to 5) that lets it rapidly "cover" a new octave. This is precisely the skill you need for fast arpeggios, that harp-like glory of the piano's sound.

(Hand Contraction-Expansion)

Cycle 8

57 JUMP-STARTS:

Play this one fast and very lightly. You will need to exert your mind and *will* behind the stresses you give the quarter notes that end each dash. This teaches you to give a minute, felt accent in the midst of a run, which helps develop controlled speed.

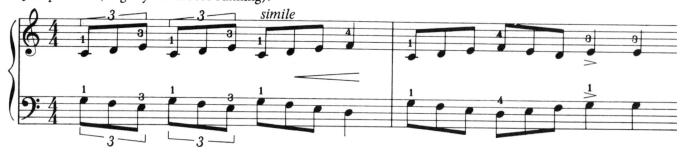

58 UP THE DOWN STAIRCASE:

"Plant" your hand well into each initial half note, then literally *melt* the next two notes together, while changing fingers. You may feel at first like a fat person wriggling out of a small window, but the agony will turn into a very pleasant flexibility of finger action.

44

Left Hand:

* Imagine your fingers as 'feet', pulling the keys towards you as they slide away beneath your hand.

HANON IN A TIZZY:

Make sure to crescendo on those repeated notes at the top of the pattern (the ones I've added to Hanon's first exercise). They are added to give you extra command over fingers 4 and 5, the ones that need special attention so that they grow equal to the stronger fingers.

60 **FLAP-DOODLES:**

By now, your thumb-tip is working along with — and as fast as — your second, fourth and fifth fingers. This exercise gives it much more to do (and consequently makes it much more alert) than any running of straight scales could.

61 **WEAVING SPELLS (RH & LH)**

Shuttling back and forth with the thumb will "oil" its action and free it well into its roots in the hand. This flexibility is very valuable for scales OR arpeggios.

Right Hand:

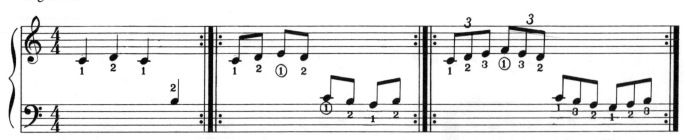

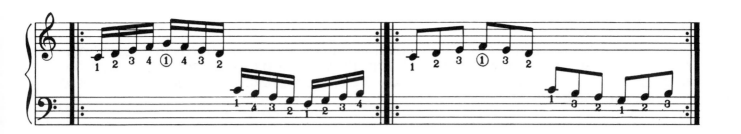

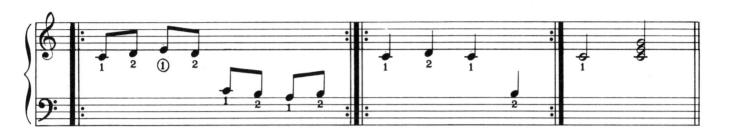

Left Hand:

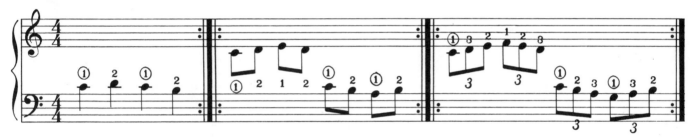

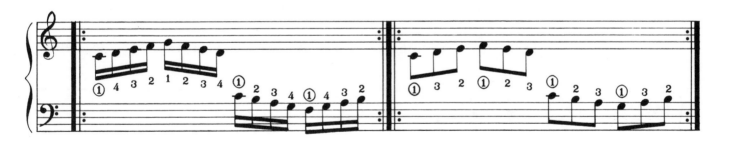

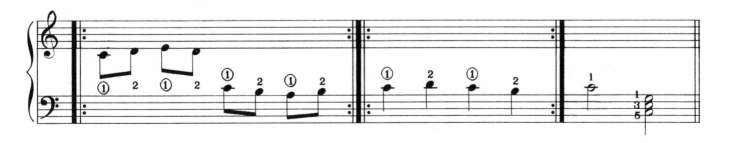

62 **MOUNTAIN CLIMB:**

Be sure to "block" or place your fingers over all the notes of the chords first, on a firm three beats per bar. This will steady and smooth your hand motion across the three octaves of the keyboard. When you then play the chords "broken," crescendo or decrescendo with the rise or fall of the pitch.

Climb - ing right up to the top of the moun - tain, (pause)

Care - ful - ly, care - ful - ly, crawl - ing back down to the val - ley.

ROCKING:

This is a useful exercise for double notes, using the fingers in their natural pairings. To get the most use, lift the wrist a little (or even lift the hand off the keys), and drop with an animal "pounce."

At each (*), stay on the keys, but up-thrust your wrist to give your "stamp of approval."

TRAIN TRIP:

This is a good ear training exercise since what you first heard as a melody is heard again, more perceptively, as a chord. Don't rush this one, and close your eyes for keener listening.

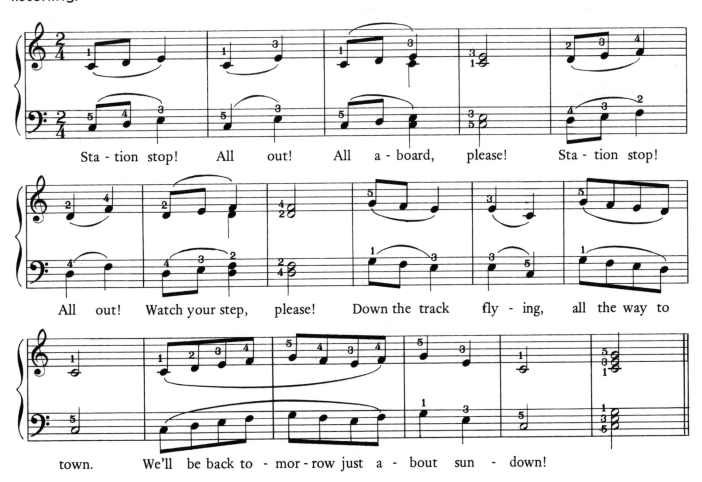

Sta - tion stop! All out! All a - board, please! Sta - tion stop!

All out! Watch your step, please! Down the track fly - ing, all the way to

town. We'll be back to - mor - row just a - bout sun - down!

65 | **TWO ON A SWING:**

This exercise further invites a natural "swing" of your wrist — an easy dip and rise with each slurred group.

Cycle 9

6

ITCHY FINGERS:

Here you combine the dip and rise of good slurring with that extra finger-ripple we call a "trill." Play the eighths neither fast nor loud, but softly and evenly. Balance your hand weight by hanging it from slightly raised wrists. Such balance will allow the fingers to fall freely onto the keys, and to work unburdened.

NOT QUITE SURE:

This is a fast-changing mixture of steps, skips and trills. You can make their interplay clear by stressing the longer note-values, and lightening the quicker ones.

Does (he/she) love me? I can't tell. When I pass (him/her) in the hall, All the but-ter-

flies in Chi-na seem to fly. When (he/she) sees me on the stair And (he/she)

just smiles stand-ing there, I could do a back-wards flip and tear my hair. Wow!

68 ## WHEELS:

For every time you try this one *legato,* try it *first non legato* (but not entirely *staccato*). Lighten your hand by letting it hang from a raised wrist. Then tap-out each note from the tips of your hanging fingers (non-legato). After that minute touch of each small note, try it more *legato.* This helps assure that in soft passages your notes do not disappear.

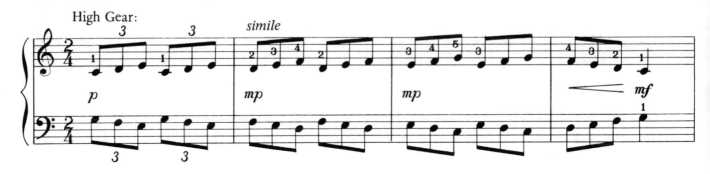

69 ## PASSING FANCY:

Play Bars 1 and 3 loudly (when you are using fingers 1,2,3,2) and softly for the lighter skill of passing 2,1,2,1. This exercise will then further refine the interaction of fingers 1 and 2 with minimal motion at their tips. You need this not only for trills, but for all ornaments in music.

52

Just ② fingers!

SKIING DOWN THE MOUNTAIN:

In this crossover exercise, keep the left hand *in place* after it has played, to serve as a marker for the right hand, which now does the traveling across the keys. Move the right hand lightly in a line as if it were suspended from the high, moving arm of a crane above your head.

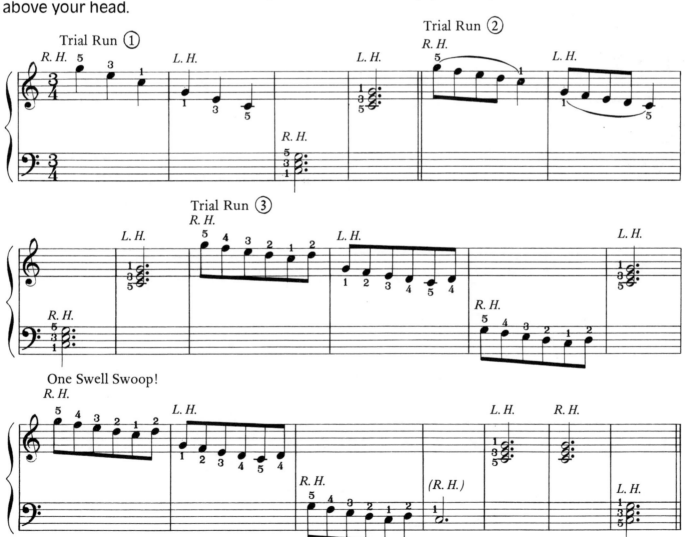

WADDLING:

First, loosen your hands by a definite, weighted accent on the first beat of every bar. Then at the "double-time" feel a resilient "spring-off" from that downbeat accent. Make only ONE accent per bar, on the downbeat.

MAKING SURE:

Here is a finger-twister step-and-skip figure that can be made perfectly clear, if you give a little sideways wobble to your hand for the following small accents:
This is a refinement of earlier exercises in rotary motion of the hand.

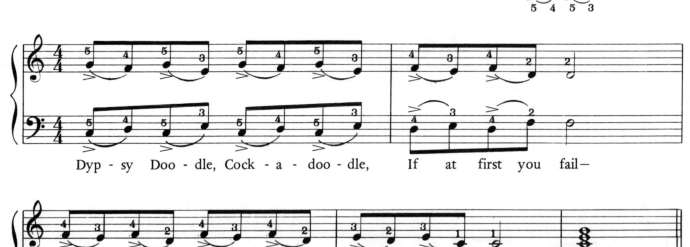

Dyp - sy Doo - dle, Cock - a - doo - dle, If at first you fail—

Try a - gain and do it bet - ter,— and you'll get the feel!

COME TO THE FAIR:

Accent 1 and 5, the "frame" fingers of the hand, and play them fast, with vigor. Then the quicker notes will subordinate themselves to those accented tones. This is good practice for Baroque ornaments.

Hi - Ho!   Come to the fair!   We're goin' to have us a   ball,   Oh boy!

Bil - ly and Bet - ty, and   Su - sy and Jim - my, and   eve - ry - one's goin' to be   there, Oh boy!

Cycle 10

74 **ROLLOVERS:**

For this exercise, keep both hands lightly balanced over the keys. Play the first note of each bar with a quick finger-flip only, free of hand weight. This is a good workout to awaken the normally sluggish fourth finger, to improve coordination through symmetrical action of both hands, and to give you the skill you need for the ornament known as a "turn."

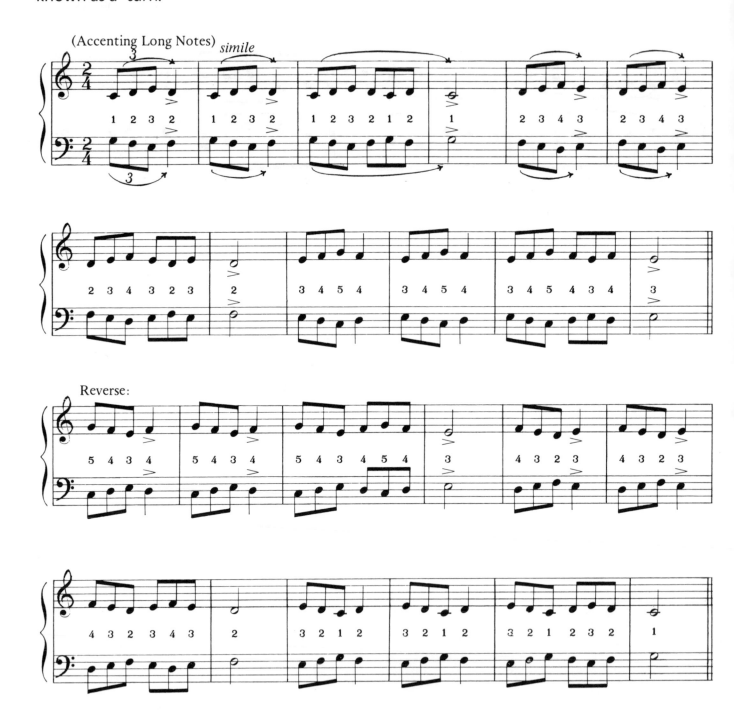

5 ## DANCING:

Exaggerate your natural dip-rise wrist action by the dynamic contrast of *F* with *P* as shown here. This contrast is intended to lead you to dip the wrist quickly (and instinctively rather than with a great weight or force) at the *forte.* Allow the hands to rise lightly (at the *piano*) from tiny little springs in your finger tips.

(At ⌢↗ dip your wrist slightly as you play, then at ↗ ↗ spring your wrist up a little, by a little pressure applied to your finger tips.)

6 ## THE MISSING LINK: TO TRIAD INVERSIONS:

Always begin this exercise with the prep-step, which forms the guideline for the scale tones. These steer the hand *by feel* from one triad inversion to the next. The point of the exercise is to use your sense of touch (eyes closed, please) to register each form of triad instantly at the touch: "Root," "First Inversion," etc.

Prep-Step: (*) It is your second or 'pointer' finger that helps you *feel* your way from one position to the next.)

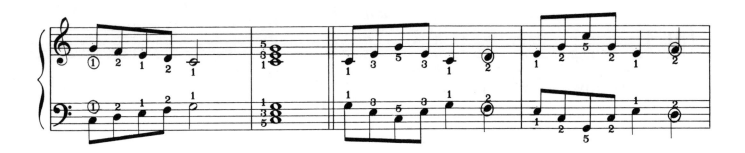

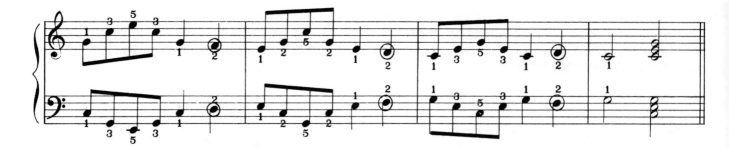

77 FLIP-FLOPS (FOR A LOOSE THUMB):

Every time you play the thumb here, shake the hand freely with it, like a soaked puppy shaking himself dry. It can help to further pry your thumb free from its locked roots in the hand.

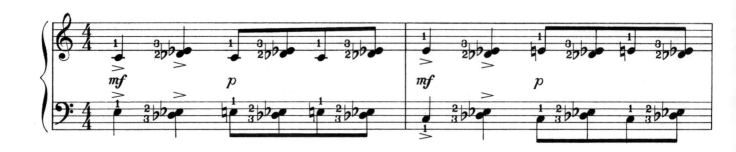

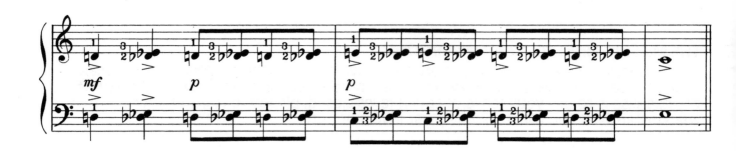

78 CADENCE CLIMBERS:

Do this exercise with a large, free, swinging back-and-forth feeling between the two hands. The tone is produced by this released hand-weight which also provides the lift-off to carry you over wide spaces of the keyboard.

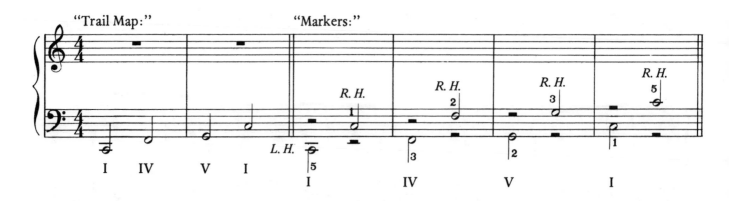

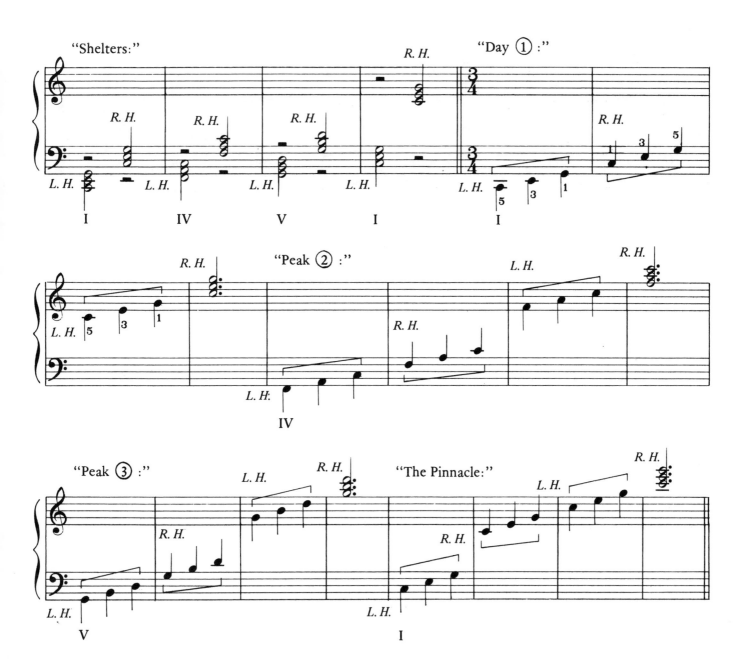

CARTWHEELS:

The first two bars of this workout must generate an easy momentum that will carry your two hands through the two-octave arpeggios of the final two octaves. "Drop and roll" you must tell yourself, to release your hand-weight into the first notes and let it carry-through the remaining notes of the chord figure. Do this one in all keys again, but *keep the same fingering* for keys beginning with black notes.

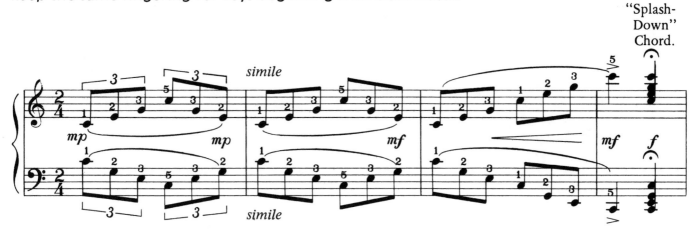

Cycle 11

BLURRED SLURS:

Dynamics are important to the shaping of a good slur. Drop-and-press into the whole note, then progressively lighten with each finger "tap" that follows on the repeated note. Thus, you show the utmost possible contrast of touch between two neighboring fingers; it's a recipe for clear, colorful "voicing" in piano writing that is thick.

DOUBLE-DATE:

In the first two bars of this exercise make a neat, deft, drop-press of the two hands, as if you meant to stencil your fingerprint into the ivory of the keys.

82 JAWS:

In this double-note exercise, the outer "frame" fingers (1 and 5 of either hand) work alternating with, or against a roving pair of inner fingers. If done deliberately, this has a beneficial massaging effect on the muscles of the under palm — muscles that need to be loosened after non-pianistic activities like driving or carrying bags. Further healthy palm-massage will occur if you play the quarter notes *forte*, and all eighth notes *piano*.

Prep-Step:

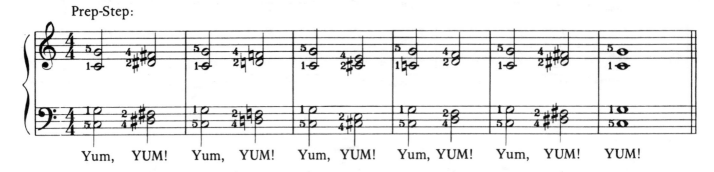

Yum, YUM!   Yum, YUM!   Yum, YUM!   Yum, YUM!   Yum, YUM!   YUM!

Big   Jaws! Gob-ble, gob-ble, Hun - gry! Gob-ble, gob-ble, Two   arms: Gob-ble, gob-ble,

Two   feet: Gob-ble, gob-ble. Two   legs: Then it eats your BOD - Y!

THUMB-BANJO: (RH & LH)

Try the first bar and you'll at once feel the open-and-shut scissors action in the inner hand that this exercise promotes. Make that action very clear by playing the quarter notes *forte,* then let the eighth notes follow *piano.* This releases stiffness in all kinds of ways. Don't hurry, work it well, in and out.

SLOW SUNDOWNS:

Let your hand weight fall freely into each of the solid triads. Then let the roll-over tendency of those hand drops propel you into the broken chords. Think as you play there, "one smooth glide," or one single stroke of a large paintbrush.

① The "Root Canal"

The sun sets (and the night falls)

Whole steps   Half   Whole steps   Half
step

② (The colors spread) - - - - - - - - - - - - - -

Build a triad on each root

③ (The wind begins to blow - - - - - -

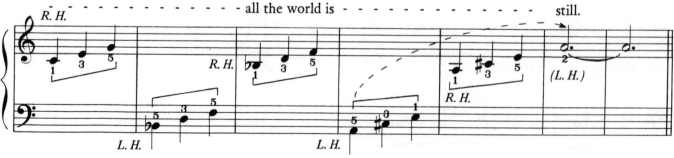

FOR OPENERS:

In this exercise, *tap* the thumb notes energetically, since that will free the rotary action of the forearm that you will need in more rapid *tremolos* later on.

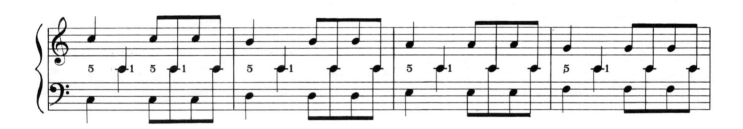

HANON GETTING DIZZY:

It is important here to *mark* the first note of each triplet very clearly. That recurrent accent will then articulate the movements of both the fifth and fourth fingers.

JUMPING-JACKS:

This exercise is intended to flex the whole hand by alternately having it reach (the "open hand"), and relax (the "closed," actually *slack* hand). Its quickening effect will work better if you go fast, but feel a distinct fingertip spring-off from the keys during each staccato touch.

② Double-Flips:

③ Triple-Flips:

INTERVAL-SPANNERS: (RH & LH)

The intention of using first and fifth fingers only for ever-changing intervals is to make those "pincer" fingers of the hand accurate in spanning melodic intervals, in bringing out the outer notes of chords, and in finding deep bass tones between chords. Practice with a definite lunge motion, to accent the fifth fingers, moving strongly away from the thumb.

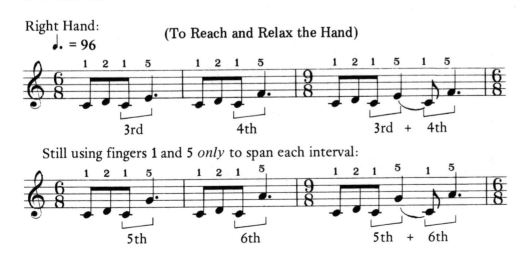

Right Hand:
$\bullet. = 96$ (To Reach and Relax the Hand)

Still using fingers 1 and 5 *only* to span each interval:

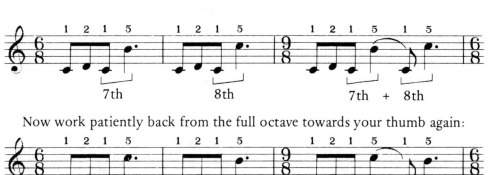

Now work patiently back from the full octave towards your thumb again:

Left Hand: (To Reach and Relax the Hand)

Now the other way:

6th   5th   6th + 5th

4th   3rd   4th + 3rd

3rd   2nd   3rd + 2nd

"Dancing on a Pinhead."

FULL-SCALE SKIDDOO'S:

The important thing to "do" here is something you cannot see: "Lie low," feeling the hand passively relaxed and inert for the whole notes. This allows it to "awaken" by moving swiftly into position for the next notes. Play the three staccato's quarter notes using your whole hand in a bouncing action, lighter with each repetition.

Right Hand:

Left Hand:

70

Cycle 12

SKATES AND BRAKES:

Since it is important to *toss* the hand freely onto the starter note of each slide-group (Bars 2, 4, 6, 8, etc.), you must first "bounce" both hands lightly but rhythmically for the opening eighths. Think of those upbeat bounces as weakening, *decrescendo,* in preparation for that quick "toss" at Bar 2.

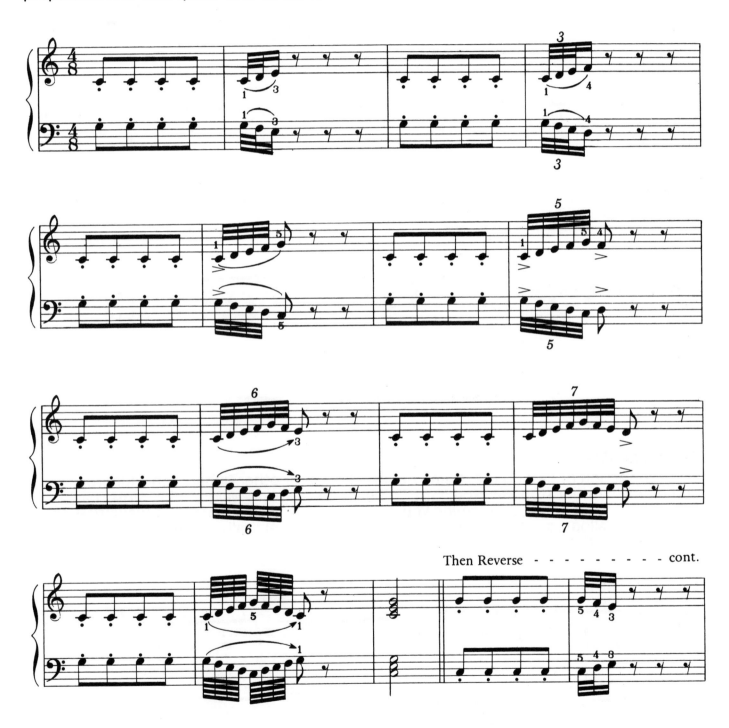

91 FIVE-FINGER BLUES:

Once again, the important thing is to deposit the hand weight into the thumbs when you drop them on beat 1 of each bar of this workout. Keep the hand-weight centered there while you let your fingers alone, free of excess heaviness, and tap out the remaining notes as true *finger* action.

92 FIGURE-SKATING:

Since the action of passing the thumb behind the tips of other fingers continues for some time without stopping, you must first balance the hand-weight (high wrist that "hangs" the hand down), and remind yourself to imagine the hand floating weightless as a hovering balloon, so that your fingers, hanging almost vertically down from the hand, easily meet and pass where their tips touch.

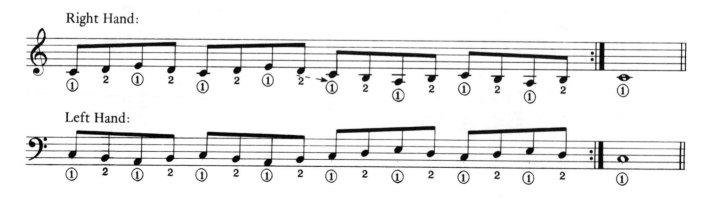

After you refine that turning motion, with fingertips movements as small and smooth as the ball bearings of your roller skates, try a wider swirl "around the bend" using 3-finger groups like this:

Right Hand:

Left Hand:

Repeat this slow twirling several times, then start again on D (using the D Major scale), and A (with scale tones of A Major). Imagine your hand as a champion skater, alone on the ice, whipping around wide "figure-eights," as a cool breeze blows around his face and hair.

ROSY FUTURE:

Step 3 is important for the reciprocal *balancing* of the hands. Feel them swaying, left to right and back, like the terminal points of a slow pendulum. Feel your hand-weight as rolling "in a sling." That imaginary "sling" would be knotted at your shoulders and wrapped around your forearms near your elbows. By centering your weight-sense there (at the elbows), it will merely "spill" into the hands as they play.

(1) Prep-step:

(2)

Root-Canal:
(Natural) minor scale

Whole Half Whole Whole Half Whole Whole
step

Now, build these triads on those roots:

am b dim C D E F G A

(3)

Now, echo each triad in the right hand:

④ Now, *let 'em roll!*

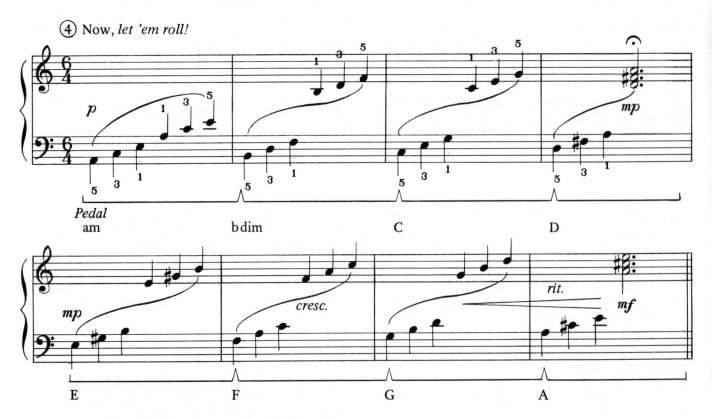

94 HOLDING THE PHONE: (THE WIRETAP BLUES)

This exercise calls for a free drop of the hand onto both thumbs; the other notes are played with the lightest (leftover) weight or mere finger action alone.

(I've Got Those Wiretap Blues)

HAND FLEXORS:

Here is another workout designed to "massage" the all-important speed muscles of the inner palm. You will get best results if you play the opening two quarter notes *forte*, followed by *piano* for the eighths immediately following. Do this one in all keys, minor as well as major, if you can.

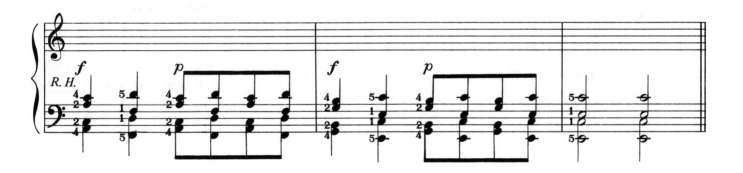

MAKING MANY WAVES:

Whichever "wave" pattern you choose, work it *with the same fingering* through every step of one octave of the given scale. Rather than simply "reciting" that scale by running it up and down, you are now doing what the composers do: building a sequence of figures that USE the steps of the scale. In every pattern start lightly and "put on the brakes," *forte,* for the final note(s) of the pattern as shown. At this point, you are actually using the scales, without having "practiced" them as such!

Play each Pattern on each step of the scale.
Then, work yourself back:

Other "Waves"

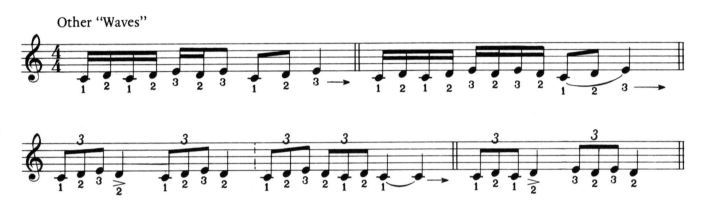